THE LITTLE BOOK OF BUDDHISM

THE LITTLE BOOK OF
BUDDHISM

HIS HOLINESS THE
DALAI LAMA

Compiled and Edited by
Renuka Singh

RIDER

LONDON · SYDNEY · AUCKLAND · JOHANNESBURG

3 5 7 9 10 8 6 4

First published in 1999 by Penguin Books India.
This edition published in 2000 by Rider,
an imprint of Ebury Press, Random House,
20 Vauxhall Bridge Road, London SW1V 2SA
www.randomhouse.co.uk

Random House Australia (Pty) Limited
20 Alfred Street, Milsons Point, Sydney,
New South Wales 2061, Australia

Random House New Zealand Limited
18 Poland Road, Glenfield,
Auckland 10, New Zealand

Random House South Africa (Pty) Limited
Endulini, 5A Jubilee Road,
Parktown 2193, South Africa

The Random House Group Limited Reg. No. 954009

Papers used by Rider are natural, recyclable products
made from wood grown in sustainable forests.

Printed and bound in Denmark by
Nørhaven A/S, Viborg

A CIP catalogue record for this book
is available from the British Library

ISBN 0-7126-0240-2

INTRODUCTION

We are the creators of our own happiness and suffering, for everything originates in the mind. So we need to take responsibility for whatever, good or bad, we experience.

This book contains the essence of Buddhism and offers practical wisdom for our daily lives in the words of His Holiness the Dalai Lama. His inspiring thoughts help to improve our state of mind, and to discover deep peace within.

This chain of Buddhist thoughts consists of pithy reflections on our need to rid ourselves of the preoccupation with mundane concerns to find refuge in Buddha, Dharma and Sangha. It teaches us the law of karma, where by living according to the Ten Virtuous Actions and the Four Noble Truths we can achieve the free heart of a Bodhisattva.

Renuka Singh

The common enemy of all religious disciplines is selfishness of mind. For it is just this which causes ignorance, anger and passion, which are at the root of all the troubles of the world.

Buddha is the teacher, Dharma is
the actual refuge and the Sangha is
the one which assists in
understanding or establishing the
objects of refuge.

When we take the Buddha as an authority, as a reliable teacher, we do so on the basis of having investigated and examined his principal teaching – the Four Noble Truths.

Whenever Buddhism has taken root in a new land, there has been a certain variation in the style in which it is observed. The Buddha himself taught differently according to the place, the occasion and the situation of those who were listening to him.

All of us have a great responsibility
to take the essence of Buddhism
and put it into practice in our
own lives.

Buddhahood is a state free of all
obstructions to knowledge and
disturbing emotions. It is the state
in which the mind is fully evolved.

From the earliest stages of our growth, we are completely dependent upon our mother's care and it is very important for us that she express her love. If children do not receive proper affection, in later life they will often find it hard to love others.

Samsara – our conditioned existence in the perpetual cycle of habitual tendencies – and nirvana – genuine freedom from such an existence – are nothing but different manifestations of a basic continuum. So this continuity of consciousness is always present. This is the meaning of tantra.

Through actual practice in
his daily life, man well fulfils the
aim of all religion, whatever
his denomination.

We can speak of an effect and a cause on the disturbing side as well as on the liberating side.

According to Buddhist practice, there are three states or steps. The initial stage is to reduce attachment towards life. The second stage is the elimination of desire and attachment to this samsara. Then in the third stage, self-cherishing is eliminated.

The three stages – birth, death and the intermediate state – are also established in terms of the subtlety of their levels of consciousness. Upon the basis of the continuity of the stream of consciousness is established the existence of rebirth and reincarnation.

Encountering sufferings will definitely contribute to the elevation of your spiritual practice, provided you are able to transform the calamity and misfortune into the path.

Faith dispels doubt and hesitation,
it liberates you from suffering and
delivers you to the city of peace
and happiness.

If subconscious anger had a parallel in Buddhist writings, it would have to do with what is called mental unhappiness or dissatisfaction. This is regarded as the source of anger and hostility. We can see subconscious anger in terms of a lack of awareness, as well as an active misconstruing of reality.

Guilt is incompatible with our thinking as you are part of an action but not fully responsible for it. You are just part of the contributing factor. However, in some cases one must repent, deliberately claim responsibility, have regret and never commit the mistake again.

In the beginning of Buddhist practice, our ability to serve others is limited. The emphasis is on healing ourselves, transforming our minds and hearts. But as we continue, we become stronger and increasingly able to serve others.

Firstly, we should re-examine our own attitude towards others and constantly check ourselves to see whether we are practicing properly. Before pointing our finger at others we should point it towards ourselves. Secondly, we must be prepared to admit our faults and stand corrected.

Suffering increases your inner strength. Also, wishing for suffering makes the suffering disappear.

Even when we are helping others
and are engaged in charity work,
we should not regard ourselves in
a very haughty way as great
protectors benefitting the weak.

An area in Tibetan Buddhism
which may be of interest to
scientists is the relationship
between the physical elements and
the nerves, in particular the
relationship between the elements
in the brain and consciousness.
This involves changes in
consciousness, happy or unhappy
states of mind, the effect they have
on the elements within the brain,
and the consequent effect that this
has on the body.

According to its level of subtlety, consciousness is classified into three levels: the waking state or gross level of consciousness; the consciousness of the dream state which is more subtle; and the consciousness during sleep, dreamless sleep, which is subtler still.

The metaphor of light is a
common image in all the major
religious traditions. In the
Buddhist context, light is
particularly associated with wisdom
and knowledge; darkness is
associated with ignorance and a
state of mis-knowledge.

In yoga tantra, the highest dimension of Buddhist practice, there is no distinction between gender. In this final life in which you attain Buddhahood, there is no difference whether you are male or female.

The creatures that inhabit this earth – be they human beings or animals – are here to contribute, each in its own particular way, to the beauty and prosperity of the world.

The Buddhist notion of attachment is not what people in the West assume. We say that the love of a mother for her only child is free of attachment.

We are born and reborn
countless number of times, and it
is possible that each being has been
our parent at one time or another.
Therefore, it is likely that all
beings in this universe have
familial connections.

The process of dying
begins with the dissolution
of the elements within the body.
It has eight stages, beginning
with the dissolution of the earth
element, then the water, fire and
wind elements. The next four
stages are visions in terms of
colour: appearance of a white
vision, increase of the red element,
black near-attainment, and finally
the clear light of death.

Do your best and do it according to your own inner standard – call it conscience – not just according to society's knowledge and judgement of your deeds.

For discovering one's true inner nature, I think one should try to take some time, with quiet and relaxation, to think more inwardly and to investigate the inner world.

When one is very involved in hatred or attachment, if there is time or possibility during that very moment, just try to look inward and ask: 'What is attachment? What is the nature of anger?'

To develop genuine devotion, you must know the meaning of teachings. The main emphasis in Buddhism is to transform the mind, and this transformation depends upon meditation. In order to meditate correctly, you must have knowledge.

Three qualities enable people to
understand the teachings:
objectivity, which means an
open mind; intelligence, which is
the critical faculty to discern the
real meaning by checking the
teachings of Buddha; and interest
and commitment, which
means enthusiasm.

Anything that contradicts
experience and logic should
be abandoned.

It is through listening that your mind will turn with faith and devotion, and you will be able to cultivate joy within your mind and make your mind stable.

Mahayana has four reliances.
First: reliance on the teaching, not
on the teacher.
Second: reliance on the
meaning, not on the words that
express it. Third: reliance on the
definitive meaning, not on the
provisional meaning.
Fourth: reliance on the
transcendent wisdom of
deep experience, not on
mere knowledge.

If we see pride among people
who have no idea about Dharma,
it is understandable. However, if
afflictive emotions and haughtiness
are present among Dharma
practitioners, it is a great disgrace
to the practice.

Individuals who are best suited for practice of Dharma are those who are not only intellectually gifted, but also have single-minded faith and dedication and are wise.

Although individuals may be highly intelligent, they are sometimes dogged by skepticism and doubts. They are clever, but they tend to be hesitant and skeptical and are never really able to settle down. These people are the least receptive.

As a spiritual trainee, you
must be prepared to endure the
hardships involved in a genuine
spiritual pursuit and be determined
to sustain your effort and will.
You must anticipate the multiple
obstacles that you are bound
to encounter along the path and
understand the key to successful
practice is never to lose
your determination.

The story of the Buddha's personal
life is the story of someone
who attained full enlightenment
through hard work
and unwavering dedication.

Laziness will stop your progress
in your spiritual practice.

When a day seems to be long, idle gossip makes our day seem shorter. But it is one of the worst ways in which we waste our time. If a tailor just holds the needle in his hand and goes on talking to a customer, the tailoring does not get finished. Besides, the needle might prick his finger. In short, meaningless gossip prevents us from doing any kind of work.

If you rely on someone who has lower qualities than yourself, that will lead to your degeneration. If you rely on someone who has qualities similar to yourself, you will stay where you are. It is only if you rely on someone who has better qualities than yourself, that you will achieve sublime status.

The advantage of relying on a spiritual teacher is that if you have accumulated an action that would project you into a negative state of existence, the result of that could be experienced just in this life in the form of minor sufferings or minor problems, or even experiencing the result in a dream and through that way one could destroy the destructive results of negative actions.

If you go more deeply into your own spiritual practice, emphasizing wisdom and compassion, you will encounter the suffering of other sentient beings again and again, and you will have the capacity to acknowledge it, respond to it and feel deep compassion rather than apathy or impotence.

When contemplating suffering, do not fall into the feeling of self-importance or conceit. Cultivating wisdom helps us to avoid these pitfalls. But it is hard to generalize because each person's courage and forbearance are unique.

The more we care for the
happiness of others, the greater is
our own sense of well-being.

A single word or expression in tantra can have four different meanings corresponding to the four levels of interpretation. These levels are known as the four modes of understanding. They are:

(i) the literal meaning;

(ii) the general meaning;

(iii) the hidden meaning; and

(iv) the ultimate meaning.

Calm abiding is a heightened state of awareness when your body and mind become especially flexible, receptive and serviceable. Special insight is also a heightened state of awareness, in which your faculty of analysis is immensely advanced. Thus calm abiding is absorptive in nature, whereas special insight is analytic in nature.

There is a true feminist movement in Buddhism. Following her attainment of bodhicitta, the goddess Tara looked upon those striving towards full awakening and she felt that there were too few women who attained Buddhahood. So she vowed, 'I have developed bodhicitta as a woman. For all of my lifetimes along the path I vow to be born as a woman, and in my final lifetime when I attain Buddhahood, then too I will be a woman.'

The problems we encounter are never the result of starting a project or work on an inappropriate day or time. Buddha always talked about negative experiences as the result of having performed negative actions. So, for a good practitioner there is no good day or bad day.

There is no way to escape death, it is just like trying to escape when you are surrounded by four great mountains touching the sky. There is no escape from these four mountains of birth, old age, sickness and death.

Ageing destroys youth, sickness destroys health, degeneration of life destroys all excellent qualities and death destroys life. Even if you are a great runner, you cannot run away from death. You cannot stop death with your wealth, through your magic performances or recitation of mantras or even medicines. Therefore, it is wise to prepare for your death.

Discipline is a supreme ornament and, whether worn by old, young or middle-aged, it gives birth only to happiness. It is perfume *par excellence* and, unlike ordinary perfumes which travel only with the wind, its refreshing aroma travels spontaneously in all directions. A peerless ointment, it brings relief from the hot pains of delusion.

Due to karmic influences, the world appears in different ways to different people. When a human being, a god and a preta – three sentient beings – look at one bowl of water, the karmic factors make the human being see it as water, while the god sees nectar and the preta sees blood.

A blossoming tree becomes bare
and stripped in autumn.
Beauty changes into ugliness,
youth into old age, and fault into
virtue. Things do not remain the
same and nothing really exists.
Thus, appearances and emptiness
exist simultaneously.

Some people who are sweet and attractive, strong and healthy, happen to die young. They are masters in disguise teaching us about impermanence.

Natural environment sustains the life of all beings universally. Trees are referred to in accounts of the principal events of Buddha's life. His mother leaned against a tree for support as she gave birth to him. He attained enlightenment seated beneath a tree, and finally passed away as trees stood witness overhead.

The Bible says that swords
can be turned into ploughshares.
It is a beautiful image, a weapon
transformed into a tool to serve
basic human needs, representing
an attitude of inner and
outer disarmament.

The true sufferings and true causes of sufferings are the effect and cause on the side of things that we do not want; the true cessation and the true paths are the effect and cause on the side of things that we desire.

The truth of suffering is that we experience many different types of suffering: suffering of suffering – things such as headaches; suffering of changes – feeling of restlessness after being comfortable; and all-pervasive suffering that acts as the basis of the first two categories and is under the control of karma and the disturbing mind.

From one point of view we can say that we have human bodies and are practicing the Buddha's teachings and are thus much better than insects. But we can also say that insects are innocent and free from guile, whereas we often lie and misrepresent ourselves in devious ways in order to achieve our ends or better ourselves. From this perspective, we are much worse than insects.

No matter who we are with, we often think things like, 'I am stronger than him', 'I am more beautiful than her', 'I am more intelligent', and so forth – we generate much pride. This is not good. Instead, we should always remain humble.

To develop patience, you need
someone who wilfully hurts you.
Such people give us the real
opportunity to practise tolerance.
They test our inner strength in a
way that even our guru cannot.
Basically, patience protects us from
being discouraged.

It is better not to avoid events or persons who annoy you and give rise to anger, if your anger is not too strong. But if the encounter is not possible, work on your anger and develop compassion by yourself.

The three physical non-virtues are killing, stealing and sexual misconduct. The four verbal non-virtues are lying, divisiveness, harsh speech and senseless speech. The three mental non-virtues are covetousness, harmful intent and wrong view.

We find that between the past and the future there is an extremely thin line – something that cannot really withstand analysis. Past and future exist in relation to the present. But if the present cannot be posited, how can past and future be posited? This is a demonstration of dependent origination.

We learn from the principle
of dependent origination that
things and events do not come
into being without causes.
Suffering and unsatisfactory
conditions are caused by our own
delusions and the contaminated
actions induced by them.

For a bodhisattva to be successful
in accomplishing the practice of
the six perfections – generosity,
ethical discipline, tolerance, joyous
effort, concentration and wisdom
– cooperation with fellow beings
and kindness towards them are
extremely important.

Suffering originates from various causes and conditions. But the root cause of our pain and suffering lies in our own ignorant and undisciplined state of mind. The happiness we seek can be attained only through the purification of our minds.

The criterion that distinguishes a school as Buddhist is its acceptance of four fundamental tenets, known as the four seals:

(i) All composite phenomena are impermanent.

(ii) All contaminated things and events are unsatisfactory.

(iii) All phenomena are empty and selfless.

(iv) Nirvana is true peace.

Vegetarianism is very admirable. However, according to Buddhism, there is no unequivocal prohibition against eating meat. What is specifically prohibited is taking any meat that you have ordered with the knowledge, or even the suspicion, that it has been killed especially for you.

Try to consider as transitory
all adverse circumstances and
disturbances. Like ripples in
a pool, they occur and
soon disappear.

Our lives are conditioned by karma. They are characterized by endless cycles of problems. One problem appears and passes, and soon another one begins.

The essence of all spiritual life
is your attitude towards others.
Once you have pure and sincere
motives all the rest follows.

You can develop the right attitude toward others if you have kindness, love and respect for them, and a clear realization of the oneness of all human beings.

It is faith that removes
mental turbidity and makes your
mind clear.

Guilt is something that can
be overcome. It does not exist in
Buddhist terminology. With the
Buddha nature, all negative things
can be purified.

In one sense, we can say it is delusion – in the form of the wisdom derived from delusions – that actually destroys itself. Similarly, it is the blissful experience of emptiness induced by sexual desire that dissolves the force of sexual impulses.

Irrespective of whether we are believers or agnostics, whether we believe in God or karma, everyone can pursue moral ethics.

Real compassion comes
from seeing the suffering of others.
You feel a sense of responsibility,
and you want to do something
for them.

Sometimes your dear friend,
though still the same person, feels
more like an enemy. Instead of
love, you feel hostility. But with
genuine love and compassion,
another person's appearance
or behaviour has no effect on
your attitude.

Ordinary compassion and love
give rise to a feeling of closeness,
but this is essentially attachment.
As long as the other person
appears to you as beautiful or
good, love remains, but as soon as
he or she appears to you as less
beautiful or good, your love
changes completely.

The teachings of Lord Buddha
comprise three graded categories
for disciplining the mind –
Shila: training in higher conduct
Samadhi: training in higher
meditation and
Prajna: training in higher wisdom.

Speech and bodily activities
which accompany mental processes
must not be allowed to run on
in unbridled and random ways.
Just as a trainer disciplines and
calms a wild and wilful steed by
rigorous and prolonged training, so
must the indiscreet and wandering
activities of body and speech be
tamed to make them docile,
righteous and skilful.

The healing power of the spirit naturally follows the path of the spirit. It abides not in the stone of fine buildings, nor in the gold of images, nor in the silk from which robes are fashioned, nor even in the paper of holy writ, but it abides in the ineffable substance of the mind and the heart of man. We should sublimate our heart's instinct and purify our thoughts.

I am talking to you and you are listening to me. We are generally under the impression that there is a speaker and an audience and there is the sound of words being spoken. But if I search within myself, I will not find the words, and if you search yourselves you will not find them either – they are all void like empty space. Yet they are not completely non-existent. This paradox relates to the dual nature of truth.

Many creatures have toiled singly
or jointly to make our lives
comfortable. The food we eat and
the clothes we wear have not just
dropped from the sky. Many
creatures have laboured to produce
them. That is why we should be
grateful to all our fellow creatures.

Compassion and loving kindness
are the hallmarks of achievement
and happiness.

If one feels very profound
compassion, this implies an
intimate connection with another
person exists already.

It is said in our scriptures that
we are to cultivate love just like
that of a mother towards her
only child.

There are many female concerns in the highest yoga tantra. For example, one of the root evils for a man is to abuse or to look down upon a woman. If a man does that, his downfall is inevitable. There is no mention of a comparable downfall for a woman who looks down on a man. So we men are jealous.

Look at one person who annoys you, and use the opportunity to counter your own anger and cultivate compassion. But if the annoyance is too powerful – if you find the person so repulsive that you cannot bear to be in his or her presence – it may be better to look for the exit!

Faith reduces your pride and is the root of veneration. With faith, you can easily traverse from one stage of the spiritual path to another.

Spiritual intimacy is necessary
for a practitioner of Buddhism,
especially when one is trying to
overcome his mental problems.

When you open yourself up
mentally, you do so only with
someone you trust from the
bottom of your heart, someone
you feel very close to. To open
yourself up in this way is an
important step in overcoming
mental problems.

The wood-born insects consume
the very wood from which they
are born. Such utilization of the
path to enlightenment is a unique
feature of tantra.

In the special dream state,
the special dream body is created
from the mind and from vital
energy within the body. This
special dream body is able to
dissociate entirely from the gross
physical body and travel elsewhere.
One way of developing this
special dream body is first of all to
recognize the dream as a dream
when it is over. Then, you find
that the dream is malleable, and
you can make efforts to gain
control over it.

In addition to practising
Buddhism in the waking state,
if you can also use your
consciousness during sleep for
wholesome purposes, then the
power of your spiritual practice
will be all the greater. Otherwise
the few hours of sleep each night
will be just a waste.

The Sutrayana method is to
cultivate a wholesome mental state
when you are going to sleep.

When the clear light nature of
the mind is veiled or inhibited
from expressing its true essence by
the conditioning of afflictive
emotions and thoughts, one is said
to be caught in samsara, the cycle
of existence. But when by
applying appropriate meditative
techniques and practices, one is
able to fully experience this state
of mind, he or she is on the
way to true liberation and
full enlightenment.

When a wrong deed has been
done, then after learning that it
was wrong, one can disclose the
deed – in the presence of actual or
imagined holy beings – and resolve
not to do that action again in
the future. This diminishes the
force of the ill deed.

Determination, courage and self-confidence are the key factors for success. If we have firm determination, we can work out obstacles and difficulties. Whatever the circumstances, we should remain humble, modest and without pride.

When you create the spiritual space and atmosphere that you are seeking through rituals and formalities, then the process will have a powerful effect on your experience. When you lack the inner dimension for that spiritual experience you are aspiring to, then rituals become mere external formalities and just a good excuse for passing time.

Blessings by themselves
are not enough. They must come
from within. Without your own
effort, it is impossible for
them to come.

There are two aspects of the path: the method aspect, which includes such practices as compassion and tolerance; and the wisdom or knowledge aspect, which involves the insight to penetrate the nature of reality. It is the latter aspect of the path that is the true antidote to dispelling ignorance.

Certain physical illnesses
improve or worsen according to
the state of mind.

It would be much
more constructive if people
tried to understand their
supposed enemies.

Learning to forgive is
infinitely more useful than merely
picking up a stone and throwing
it at the object of one's anger,
especially when the provocation
is extreme.

The grosser consciousness depends heavily on particles of matter. The subtler consciousness is more independent – it does not depend so much on the brain. In the Buddha state, the grosser mind completely disappears. Luminance, radiance, imminence – the three states of subtle mind – disappear in the clear light of the innermost consciousness.

What is reborn are our habits.
Enlightenment is the ending
of rebirth, which means
complete non-attachment or
non-identification with all
thought, feeling, perception,
physical sensations
and ideas.

The observation that good people suffer and evil people enjoy success and recognition is short-signed. Also this conclusion might have been drawn in haste. If one analyses carefully, one finds that troublemakers are definitely not happy. It is better to behave well, take responsibility for one's actions, and lead a positive life.

The greatest degree of
inner tranquility comes from
the development of love
and compassion.

Cultivating closeness and warmth for others automatically puts the mind at ease. It is the ultimate source of success in life.

True compassion is not just
an emotional response but a firm
commitment founded on reason.
Therefore, a truly compassionate
attitude towards others does
not change even if they
behave negatively.

Through universal altruism,
you develop a feeling of
responsibility for others and
the wish to help them actively
overcome their problems.

One should practise spirituality with a motivation similar to that of a child fully absorbed in play. Such a child is so delighted and engrossed in what he is doing that he never feels satisfied or tired. Such should be your mental attitude when practising Dharma.

If a person has a really deep interest in spiritual growth, he or she cannot do away with the practice of meditation. That is the key to spiritual growth.

Mere prayer or a wish
will not affect inner spiritual
change. The only way for
development is by constant effort
through meditation.

In the beginning practice
is not easy. You may encounter
difficulties or experience a loss of
enthusiasm. Or perhaps there will
be too much enthusiasm – then
after a few weeks or months,
your enthusiasm may wane. You
need to develop a constant
persistent approach based on a
long-term commitment.

In the quest for mental quiescence, there is a state where striving must be abandoned, for an effortless concentration is necessary. Your mind then becomes very tranquil and achieves a state of wholeness. At that moment, to make an effort would disturb that pure tranquility.

So in order to maintain that tranquility, effortless effort must be used.

Such practices as bodhicitta automatically bring calm at the time of death. The mind is then at a very critical period. If you are able to create a strong positive impact at that time, then this becomes a very powerful force in continuing that positive influence in the next life.

We practise various meditations in dream states. The virtue of such practices is that during such states, it is possible to separate the gross levels of consciousness from the gross physical state, and arrive at a subtler level of mind and body.

The teacher is responsible
for his or her improper behaviour.
It is the student's responsibility
not to be drawn into it. The
blame is on both: the student,
because he is too obedient and
devoted to the teacher; and the
teacher, because he lacks the
integrity necessary to be immune
to that kind of vulnerability.

If there is love, there is hope
that one may have real families,
real brotherhood, real equanimity,
real peace. If the love within your
mind is lost and you see other
beings as enemies, then no
matter how much knowledge
or education or material comfort
you have, only suffering and
confusion will ensue.

Human beings will continue to deceive and overpower one another. Basically, everyone exists in a state of suffering, so to abuse or mistreat each other is futile. The foundation of all spiritual practice is love. That you practise this well is my only request.

'To do our best' means that at all times in our everyday life we should probe our minds so that we don't feel guilty about our mistakes, even though others don't know about them. If we do that, we are truly doing our best.

One can be deceived by three types of laziness: the laziness of indolence, which is the wish to procrastinate; the laziness of inferiority, which is doubting your capabilities; and the laziness that is attachment to negative actions, or putting great effort into non-virtue.

Listening cultivates wisdom and removes ignorance. It is like a torch that dispels ignorance. If you enrich your mental continuum by listening, no one can steal that wealth. It is the supreme wealth.

Every noble work is bound to encounter problems and obstacles. It is important to check your goal and motivation thoroughly. One should be very truthful, honest and reasonable. One's action should be good for others, and for oneself as well.

Emptiness should be understood in the context of dependent arising and it should evoke a sense of fullness, of things created by causes and conditions. We should not think that the self is something that was originally there and can be eliminated through meditation. In fact, the self is something that never existed in the first place.

To help others in
vast and extensive ways we
need to have attained one of
the levels of Bodhisattva, that is,
to have experienced the direct
non-conceptual reality of voidness
and to have achieved the power
of extra-sensory perception.

Our state of mind plays a major role in our day-to-day experiences as well as in our physical and mental well-being. If a person has a calm and stable mind, this influences his or her attitude and behaviour in relation to others. In other words, if someone exists in a peaceful and tranquil state of mind, external surroundings can cause them only a limited disturbance.

It is under the greatest adversity
that there exists the greatest
potential for doing good, both for
oneself and others.

About the Author

Tenzin Gyatso,
His Holiness the fourteenth
Dalai Lama
is the spiritual and temporal leader
of the Tibetan people. He has
written several books on Buddhism
and philosophy, and has received
many international awards,
including the 1989 Nobel Prize
as recognition for his advocacy
of world peace and
inter-religious understanding.

ABOUT THE EDITOR

Renuka Singh is well-known in the field of Buddhist studies. She has edited *The Dalai Lama's Book of Daily Meditations* and *The Transformed Mind*.